W9-AUS-322

Dedication

This book is dedicated to my parents
who raised me to be a positive person
and who encouraged me to be my best.
It is also dedicated to my husband, Lee,
and daughter, Audra, who have
supported me through the years.

Thanks

I would like to thank Debra Nettles and
Leisure Arts for providing me with the
opportunity to share my unique finishes
with you.

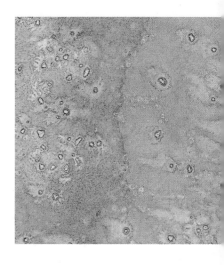

Production Team: Technical Editor – Jennifer S. Hutchings; Senior Graphic Artist – Chaska Richardson Lucas; Graphic Artists – Karen F. Allbright and Autumn Hall; and Photography Stylist – Karen Hall.

The information in this publication is presented in good faith, but no warranty is given, nor results guaranteed. Since we have no control over physical conditions surrounding the application of information herein contained, Leisure Arts, Inc., disclaims any liability for untoward results.

If you enjoy decorative art and sharing painting ideas with others, you should join the Society of Decorative Painters, a unique and exciting organization of enthusiastic painters. For more information, write to: SDP, 393 N. McLean Blvd., Wichita, KS 67203-5968. Or call (316) 269-9300 or visit their website at www.decorativepainters.org.

GENERAL PAINTING SUPPLIES

The supplies used to reproduce the finishes in this book are relatively inexpensive and are available in many discount stores, craft shops, and hardware departments. Acrylic paint colors and additional supplies needed to achieve each finish are included with individual finish instructions.

Delta Ceramcoat® acrylic paints
Delta Ceramcoat® Faux Glaze Base
Delta Ceramcoat® All-Purpose Sealer
Delta Ceramcoat® Interior/Exterior Varnish
Paintbrushes – a stiff bristle brush or toothbrush,
    various-size chip brushes, a script brush for lines
    or veining marble, and paint rollers and handles
Sponges – sea sponges and cellulose kitchen sponges

Foam plates or paint trays
Painter's tape
Measuring spoons or measuring cups – for measuring
    paint and glaze mixtures
Water containers
Rags or disposable lint-free towels
Sandpaper
Tack cloth

PAINT AND PRODUCTS

The finishes in this book are painted with non-toxic, water-based Delta Ceramcoat® acrylic paints. Interior finish latex paint may be substituted for larger projects. You **must** mix faux glaze with latex paint. Faux glaze is also often mixed with acrylic paints.

FAUX GLAZE

Faux glaze allows paint to remain workable longer and may be added to paint in various amounts or used alone. Glaze may also be used to mount papers to surfaces. I mixed Delta Ceramcoat® Faux Finish Glaze Base with some of the acrylic paints in this book. Faux glaze for latex paints can be purchased where latex paints are sold.

SEALER/PRIMER

It is necessary to use sealer/primer when you paint on a porous surface. I used Delta Ceramcoat® All-Purpose Sealer for the projects in this book. Begin by sanding your surface, then wipe off sanding dust with a tack cloth. Follow manufacturer's instructions to apply a coat of sealer to your project; allow the sealer to dry. Finish by lightly sanding your surface again.

VARNISHES

Painted finishes on furniture and decorator items need an extra layer of protection. Water-based varnishes are very durable and will enhance the appearance of your decorative treatments. I used Delta Ceramcoat® Interior/Exterior Varnish, which is available in a gloss or a satin finish, to varnish the projects in this book.

BASIC PAINTING TECHNIQUES

SPECKLING

Speckling can add texture to a finish. It can also be used to soften the underlying base colors on your project. Use a stiff toothbrush or bristle brush to speckle your surface. Begin by dipping the brush in water, then mix the water into the desired paint color with the brush bristles. Place the bristles over your surface and run your finger or a craft stick across the bristles. If your paint is too dry, the paint with not leave specks. If your paint is too wet, large spots of color are left behind. Remember less speckling is better than too much.

SPECKLING

SPONGING

Sponging is a technique that will create a unique texture on your surface. I used sea sponges and kitchen sponges in this book. Sea sponges provide a wonderful texture. Use a sea sponge and the stippling technique, page 10, to create a wonderful finish. Kitchen sponges can also create unique effects depending on the type of sponge and the technique used. One way to use a kitchen sponge is to gently set a damp sponge on a wet color layer and lift off some of the color, page 5. Another way is to apply color directly to the sponge and lightly press the sponge impression onto your surface. Vary the angle of your sponges as you apply them to your surface to provide more interesting textures. You will need to clean sponges often to keep clean impressions.

STIPPLING TECHNIQUE USING A SEA SPONGE

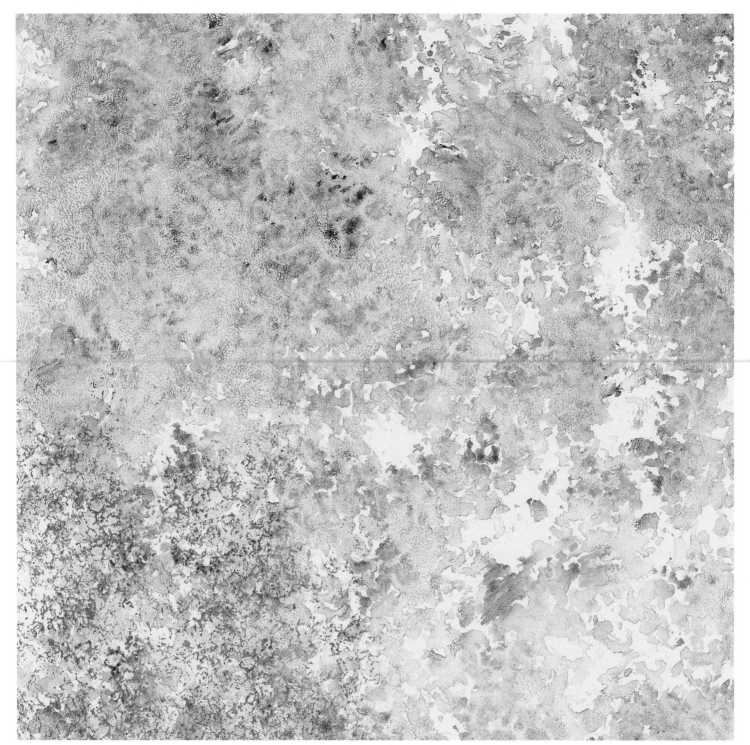

ALCOHOL DROPS

Dropping rubbing alcohol on a wet paint surface creates a unique pattern. Alcohol may be applied using the speckling technique, page 3, or it can simply be dropped onto your surface depending on the pattern size desired. This technique is done using a stiff toothbrush. (Using a toothbrush will allow you to have some control on how much alcohol will be dropped onto your surface.) Light speckling will create a fine spotty texture. Large drops provide larger areas of texture and may be formed by shaking the toothbrush over your surface or by tapping the toothbrush against your opposite hand. Repeated speckling will create a less obvious pattern. Remember the paint on your surface has to be wet for this technique to work – if the paint is too dry, no patterns will form. Also keep in mind that alcohol will soften paint layers on surfaces, so approach any manual manipulation with tools carefully!

ALCOHOL DROPS – LIGHT SPECKLES

ALCOHOL DROPS – LARGE DROPS

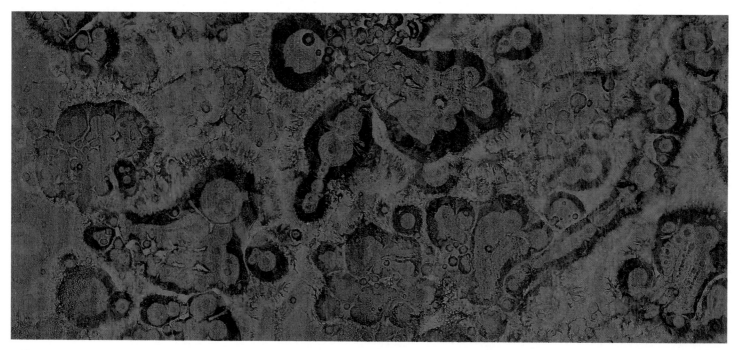

SALTING

Kosher salt applied to wet paint creates unusual patterns as it melts. Begin by applying color to your surface. While the paint is still wet, drop a few salt crystals on the surface. Water may be sprayed onto the salted areas of your surface for even different effects, this page and page 8. Allow each layer to dry completely, then remove the salt by gently wiping your surface with a dry rag. Keep in mind that exact pattern duplication is difficult. You can repeat the steps to add more pattern layers. Another interesting effect is to apply alcohol drops, page 6, and salt while the paint on your surface is wet, page 9.

SALTING – LIGHTLY SPRAYED WITH WATER

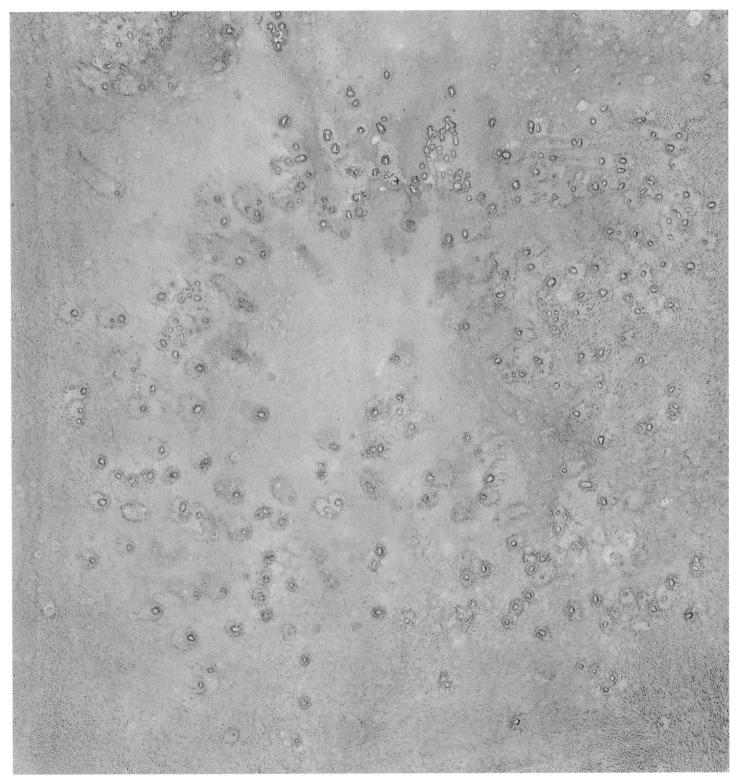

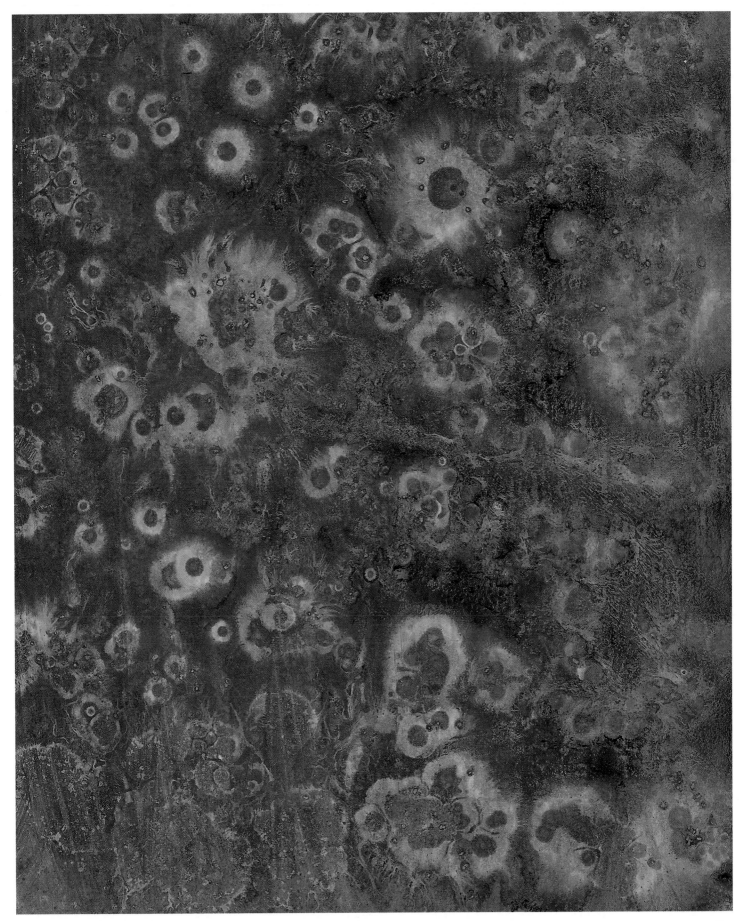

GLAZING

Glazing allows a new color to be applied over an existing color to alter that color or it allows a new layer to be added. Faux glaze may also be used as barrier between paint layers to create more depth. Faux glaze allows paint to remain workable longer and can be mixed with paint if desired. The amount of glaze added to your paint will determine the transparency of your glaze. Begin this technique with a chip brush loaded in the desired color mixed with faux glaze. Brush the mixture evenly over your surface. Now you are ready to complete the desired finish technique. Allow each glaze layer to dry completely before applying another color.

VEINING

Veining is a technique used in marbling. Veins are made using a script brush. Begin by thinning the desired vein color with water. The paint should be thin enough to release from your brush easily, leaving a nice flowing line without skipping. Load the brush with paint, then place the brush parallel to your surface. Slowly roll the brush handle back and forth between your thumb and index finger while pulling the brush across surface towards you. Keep in mind that most marble veins pass diagonally across the surface. Lightly spritz the surface with water to soften veins. If the veins are too dominant, lightly sponge over them with the marble color. Remember less veining is better than too much. Keep your project size in mind – larger projects can support a busier finish.

STIPPLING

Stippling is another commonly used technique used to add texture to a finish. Stippling is a technique where paint is tapped onto the surface using a light up and down motion. This can be done with brushes or sponges. Begin by dipping the desired tool into paint, then tap the loaded tool on the surface. Light tapping will produce a light application of color. Heavier pressure will "mash" color into the surface and cover the area more solidly. Repeated stippling in the same area may result in over-blended colors, which produces a less interesting pattern. If this happens, allow stippling to dry, basecoat the area with the original color, allow this to dry, then stipple the area again with the desired color.

SPRITZING

Spray bottles are available in many styles. Fine mist sprayers are great for spritzing water on your surface to soften or blur paint patterns. Trigger sprayers will provide a choice in spray patterns and will produce a more aggressive liquid release.

BLENDING

Many finishes would be very busy without blending. Paint needs to be blended where edges are harsh or where two colors touch and leave an undesirable pattern. Blending is done with brushes, sponges, and water. Use a little faux glaze as a blending aid, if desired.

DIRECT PAINT APPLICATION

Direct paint application is a technique where paint is placed on a tool, then the tool is placed on the surface to leave a print. This technique is often referred to as "positive painting."

PAINT REMOVAL

Paint removal is a technique where paint is applied to the surface, then the paint is manipulated with a tool to lift the paint from the surface to create texture. This technique is often referred to as "negative painting."

DRY BRUSHING

Dry brushing provides texture with color. Chip brushes or coarse bristle brushes work best for this technique. Begin the process by lightly touching a clean, dry brush to your paint, then remove most of the paint on a rag or towel. Lightly pass the bristles of the brush over the desired surface in a dusting motion. The desired result is a gradual build up of thin paint layers. Your surface will feel gritty or dusty when it is painted correctly. Your brushes need to be cleaned frequently because dry paint will build up on the brush bristles, making the technique difficult to complete properly. Remember that your brush must be dry to produce this finish. You may find it helpful to use more than one brush.

STONE *Finishes*

GRANITE

Granite is a fun finish to create. You will use stippling, along with spritzing and speckling, to create this finish. Keep in mind that granite colors vary and you can select paint colors to coordinate with your home décor items.

PALETTE:

Delta Ceramcoat® Acrylics
Autumn Brown
Black or Black Green
Chamomile
Dark Victorian Teal

SUPPLIES:

Water bottle

Read the General Painting Supplies and Basic Painting Techniques, pages 2-10, before you begin to paint.

GRANITE FINISH

1. Basecoat the surface with Chamomile; allow the paint to dry.
2. Lightly spritz the surface with water. Mix Black or Black Green and glaze (1:1) on a foam plate. Pick up the mixture on a sea sponge. Using the loaded sponge, lightly stipple the surface, leaving some of the light background color visible (Fig. 1). If you think the surface looks too patterned, lightly spritz it with water. Allow the paint to dry.
3. Mix Dark Victorian Teal and glaze (1:1) on a foam plate. Pick up the mixture on a clean sea sponge and stipple the surface with a small amount of the mixture (Fig. 2). (Remember – small amounts of color are plenty for this finish.) Spritz the surface with a little water. Allow the paint to dry.
4. Repeat step 3 using Chamomile, then Autumn Brown (Fig. 3, page 14).

FIG. 1

Instructions continued on page 15

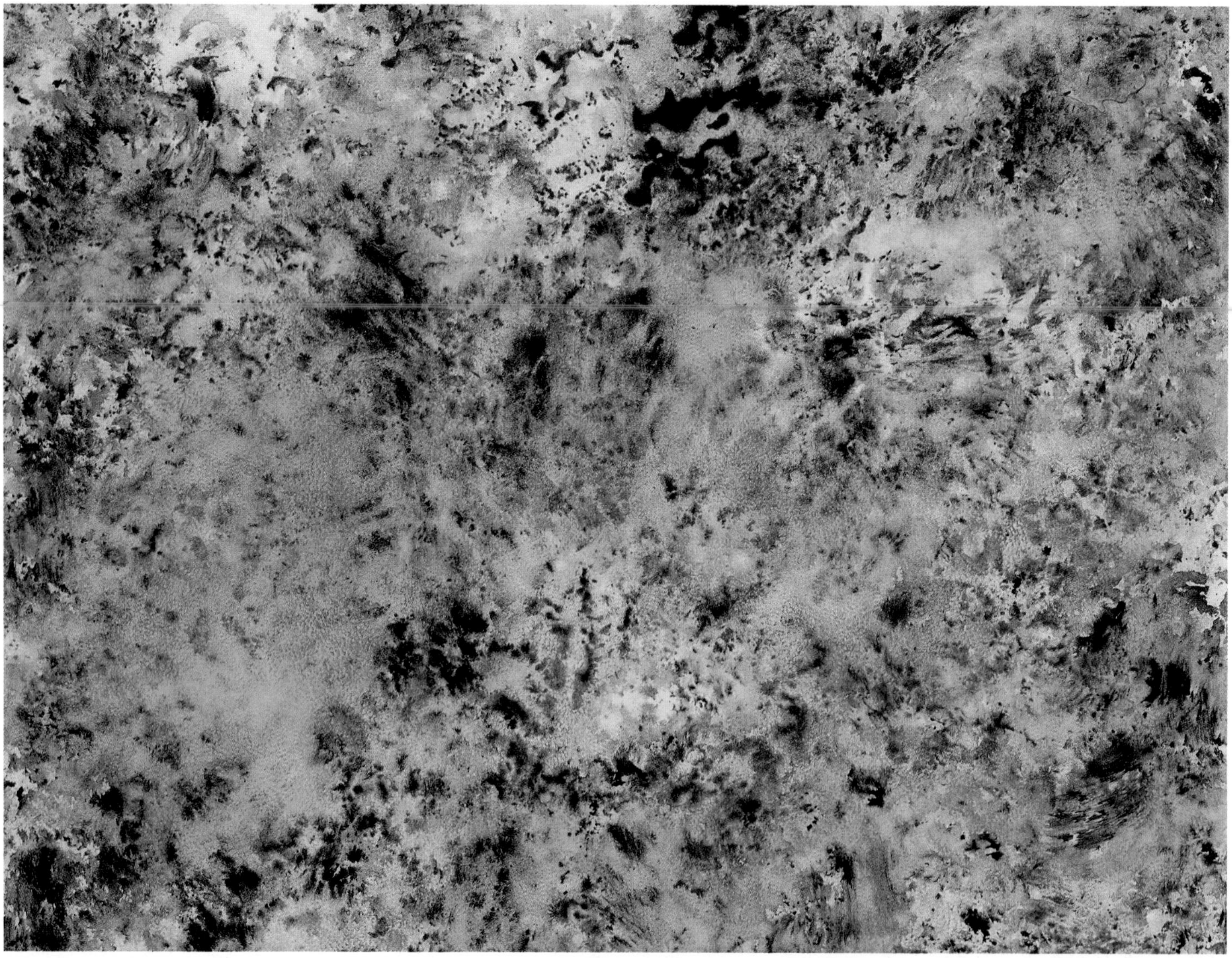

FIG. 2

FIG. 3

5. It may be necessary to stipple in a few fresh black areas. Lightly spritz the surface with water and allow the surface to dry.
6. Use a toothbrush and speckle the surface with Autumn Brown and Black (Fig. 4).
7. Try this technique with other color combinations, such as with shades of brown (Fig. 5).

FIG. 4

FIG. 5

LIGHTLY TEXTURED STONE

Many times faux finishes require you to combine paint techniques to produce the desired look. For this finish, you will use the alcohol drops, salting, and spritzing techniques. You will also use a hair dryer to "move" color around on your surface.

PALETTE:

Delta Ceramcoat® Acrylics
Butter Cream
Chamomile
Dark Foliage Green
Dark Victorian Teal
Pigskin

SUPPLIES:

Rubbing alcohol
Kosher salt
Hair dryer

Read the General Painting Supplies and Basic Painting Techniques, pages 2-10, before you begin to paint.

LIGHTLY TEXTURED STONE FINISH

1. Basecoat the surface with Butter Cream; allow the paint to dry.
2. Mix Dark Foliage Green, glaze, and water (1:2:2) on a foam plate. (The paint mixture will be an inky consistency.) Brush the mixture over your surface; set aside mixture. Sprinkle a small amount of kosher salt onto the wet surface. Now, drop a few drops of rubbing alcohol onto the wet surface. Use the hair dryer to "move" the color to the desired areas on the surface (Fig. 1). Allow the paint to dry.

FIG. 1

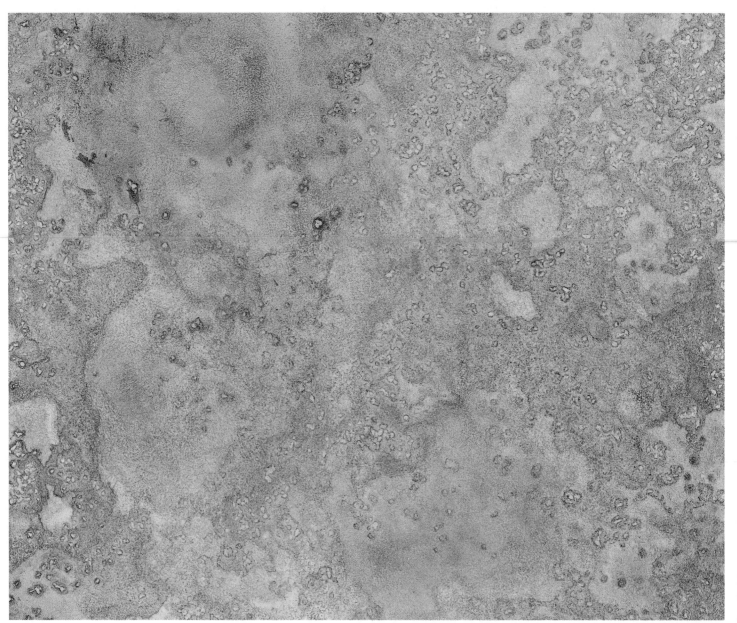

3. Remove the salt from the dry surface. Brush or roll on a layer of varnish and allow it to dry. (This creates a barrier layer and adds depth to your finish.)
4. Mix Dark Victorian Teal, glaze, and water (1:2:2) on a foam plate. (The paint mixture will be an inky consistency.) Repeat step 2 with this mixture (Fig. 2). Allow the paint to dry.

5. Remove the salt from the dry surface. Brush or roll on another layer of varnish and allow it to dry.
6. Mix Pigskin, glaze, and water (1:2:2) on a foam plate. (The paint mixture will be an inky consistency.) Repeat step 2 with this mixture (Fig. 3). Allow the paint to dry. Remove the salt from the dry surface.

Instructions continued on page 18

FIG. 2

FIG. 3

7. Repeat step 2 again using very thin layer of the Dark Foliage Green glaze from step 2. Mix Chamomile, glaze, and water (1:2:2) on a foam plate. Repeat step 2 using a very thin layer of the Chamomile glaze (Fig. 4). Allow the paint to dry. For a different look, use less salt (Fig. 5).

8. Apply several coats of varnish to the surface according to product directions.

FIG. 5

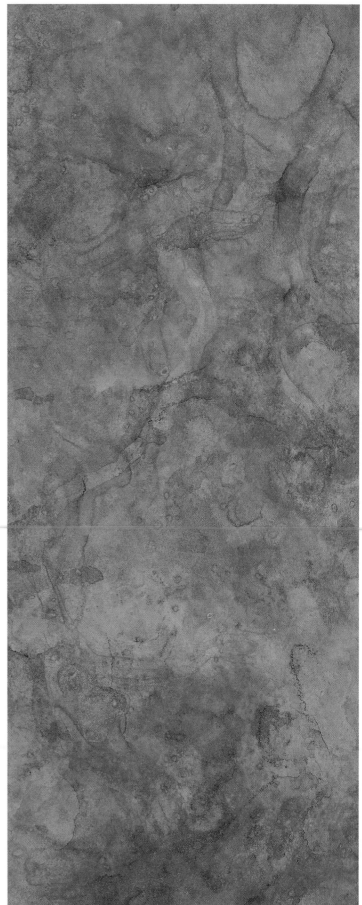

FIG. 4

MARBLE

Mother Nature has provided us with wonderful marble types. The look of marble will differ depending upon the minerals in the stone and environmental interaction with the stone. Marble types and colors are numerous in nature, with some that are veined and some that aren't. There are many techniques that can be used to replicate the look of marble. I use both the direct paint application and paint removal techniques in this book. I also combine some of the basic techniques and use different tools to apply the paint to create some of the interesting variations.

BANDED ROLLER MARBLING

This finish is achieved using a tool called a banded roller. The handmade roller tool is made by randomly wrapping various widths of rubber bands around a plastic water bottle (Fig. 1). The roller doesn't have to be completely covered in rubber bands. After you have wrapped several rubber bands around your roller, test the roller pattern with paint on a piece of newspaper to check the patterning – you may want to add more rubber bands or you may want to take some off of the roller. You can use this roller for the direct paint application or paint removal techniques, or you can mix the techniques together.

PALETTE:
Delta Ceramcoat® Acrylics
Butter Cream
Candy Bar Brown
Dunes Beige

SUPPLIES:
Banded roller (see italic note to construct)

Read the General Painting Supplies and Basic Painting Techniques, pages 2-10, before you begin to paint.

Instructions continued on page 20

FIG. 1

BANDED ROLLER MARBLING FINISH – DIRECT PAINT APPLICATION TECHNIQUE

1. Basecoat the surface with Butter Cream; allow the paint to dry.
2. Mix Candy Bar Brown and glaze (1:1) on a foam plate. (Add a little more glaze to the mixture if you would like a thinner, lighter color.) Pick up the mixture on a chip brush and brush the color over the rubber bands on your roller. Begin rolling the roller in all directions on your surface until you obtain the desired patterning (Fig. 2). "Reload" your roller with paint as often as needed and clean the roller often with a damp sponge to keep the pattern crisp. Allow the paint to dry.

3. Now you can add more colors to the marble finish if you'd like. Mix Dunes Beige and glaze (1:1) on a foam plate, then use your chip brush to apply the mixture to your roller. Roll the roller across the surface until the desired effect is achieved (Fig. 3). You can keep adding layers of color as long as contrast still shows between your colors. Allow the paint to dry.

FIG. 2

FIG. 3

BANDED ROLLER MARBLING FINISH – PAINT REMOVAL TECHNIQUE, MIXED TECHNIQUES

1. Basecoat the surface with Butter Cream; allow the paint to dry.
2. Mix Candy Bar Brown and glaze (1:1) on a foam plate. Brush a layer of the mixture onto the surface. While the paint is still wet, take a clean, dry banded roller and roll it across the wet surface, being sure to vary the direction as you roll (Fig. 4). Clean the roller often with a damp sponge to keep the pattern crisp. The more that you roll across the surface, the softer the effect will be. Allow the paint to dry.

3. You can now add another layer of color by using the direct paint application technique. Mix Dunes Beige and glaze (1:1) on a foam plate, then use your chip brush to apply the mixture to your banded roller. Roll the roller across the surface until the desired effect is achieved (Fig. 5).

FIG. 4

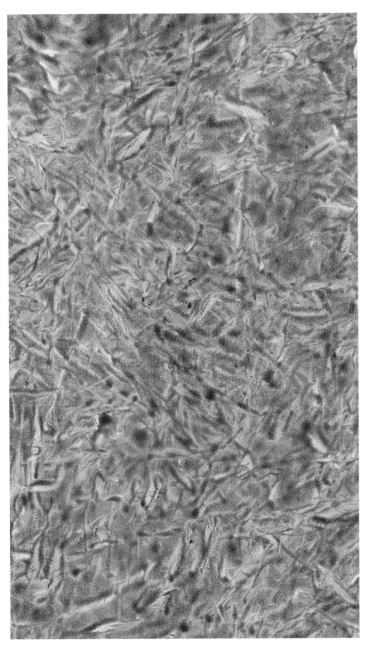

FIG. 5

PLASTIC WRAP MARBLING

This marbling finish is fun to create because the patterns happen almost magically. Plastic wraps and plastic shopping bags are used as tools to paint this finish. Different types of plastics will give you different patterning. Thick plastics will leave coarser patterns, while thin wraps will leave a finer pattern. Also, some plastics will maintain wrinkles, while others do not. I used both the direct paint application and the paint removal techniques for this finish.

PALETTE:

Delta Ceramcoat® Acrylics
Butter Cream
Desert Sun Orange
Medium Victorian Teal
Maple Sugar Tan

SUPPLIES:

Plastic wrap or thin plastic shopping bags

Read the General Painting Supplies and Basic Painting Techniques, pages 2-10, before you begin to paint.

PLASTIC WRAP MARBLING FINISH – DIRECT PAINT APPLICATION TECHNIQUE

1. Basecoat the surface with Butter Cream; allow the paint to dry.
2. Select piece of plastic wrap or plastic shopping bag. Make sure the printing is turned to the inside and wad plastic piece into a ball in your hand. This will be your paint tool. Keeping the plastic wadded into a ball, dip the plastic into Desert Sun Orange. Remove the excess paint on a foam plate. Using the plastic tool, lightly stipple the surface, leaving some of the light background color visible (Fig. 6). Change your plastic piece often to ensure crisp patterning. Allow the paint to dry.
3. Mix Medium Victorian Teal and glaze (1:1) on a foam plate. Select a new plastic piece and wad it into a ball. Dip the plastic into the mixture, then stipple over the desired areas of your surface (Fig. 7). Allow the paint to dry.

FIG. 6

Instructions continued on page 24

FIG. 7

PLASTIC WRAP MARBLING FINISH – PAINT REMOVAL TECHNIQUE

1. Basecoat the surface with Butter Cream; allow the paint to dry.
2. Mix Desert Sun Orange or Dark Victorian Teal and glaze (1:1) on a foam plate. Brush a layer of the mixture onto the surface. Wrinkle up a piece of plastic with the printing to the inside. Open the plastic sheet and press it onto the surface, allowing wrinkles to form. Carefully remove plastic by lifting it straight up, then discard it. (Notice how the pattern varies between the stiffer plastic used in Fig. 8 and softer store brand plastic wrap used in Fig. 9). Allow the paint to dry. Be sure to begin each section with a fresh plastic sheet.

FIG. 9

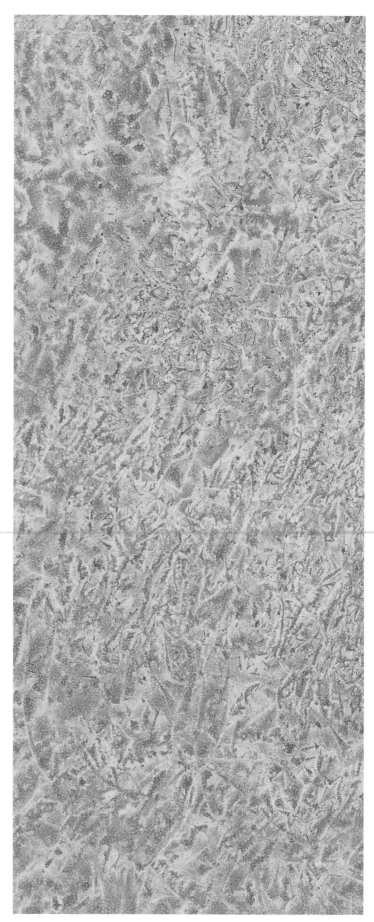

FIG. 8

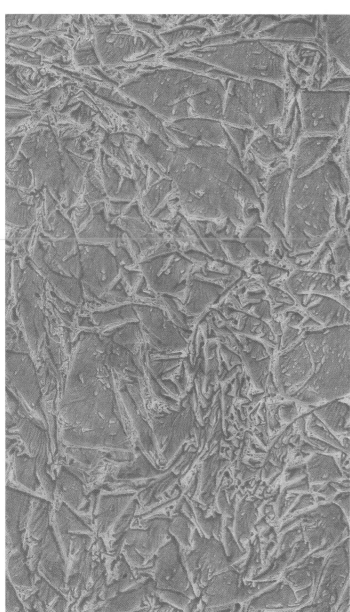

FIG. 11

3. Now you can add more colors to the marble finish if you'd like, just allow each glazed area to dry before a new layer of color is applied. Mix Dark Victorian Teal and glaze and Maple Sugar Tan and glaze (1:1 each) on a foam plate, then refer to step 2 to add a layer of Dark Victorian Teal (Fig. 10) and a layer of Maple Sugar Tan (Fig. 11).

FIG. 10

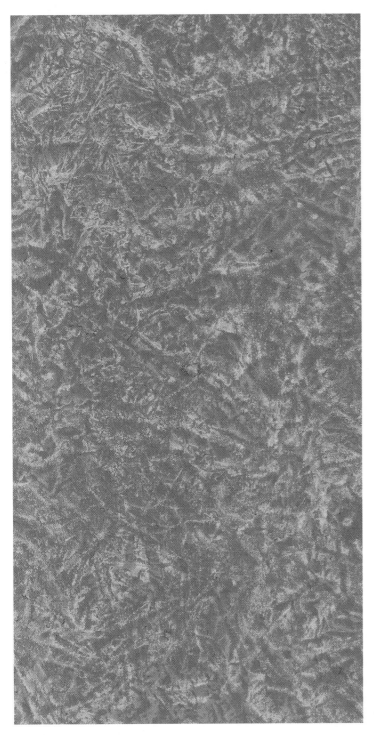

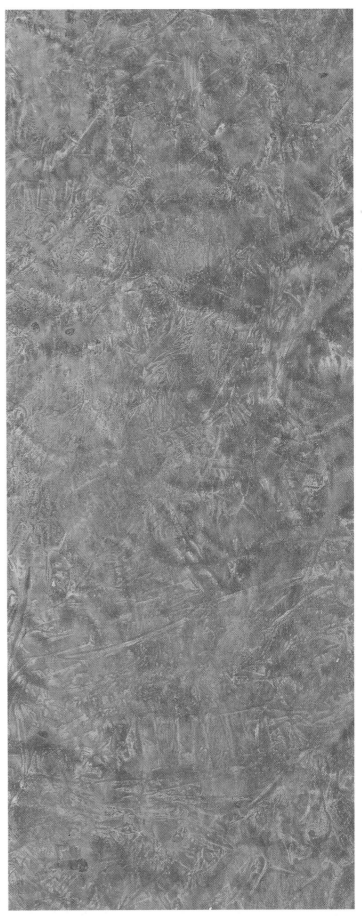

SPONGE MARBLING

Sea sponges provide good texture when creating a sponge marbling finish. You can add depth to your finish by stippling the surface with a variation of colors.

PALETTE:

Delta Ceramcoat® Acrylics
Butter Cream
Pink Quartz

SUPPLIES:

Water bottle
Hair dryer

Read the General Painting Supplies and Basic Painting Techniques, pages 2-10, before you begin to paint.

SPONGE MARBLING FINISH

1. Basecoat the surface with Butter Cream; allow the paint to dry.
2. Mix Pink Quartz and glaze (1:1) on a foam plate. Lightly spritz the surface with water. Pick up the mixture on a damp sea sponge. Using the sponge, lightly stipple the surface, leaving some of the light background color visible. Spritz the surface with water again. Your paint will become quite thin and may begin to move across the surface. You can use the hair dryer to "move" the paint around to the desired areas and to begin drying the paint puddles but don't use it to completely dry the surface.
3. While the paint is still wet, pick up more of the paint mixture on your sponge, and stipple more color onto the surface (Fig. 12). Allow the paint to dry.

FIG. 12

VEINED MARBLING

Many marbled stones contain fine lines or cracks that develop as the stone is formed. These areas are referred to as veins. You will need to use several of the basic paint techniques to paint the background of this marbled finish and you will use a script brush to paint the veins on the background.

PALETTE:

Delta Ceramcoat® Acrylics
Black
Butter Cream
Dark Foliage Green

SUPPLIES:

Water bottle

Read the General Painting Supplies and Basic Painting Techniques, pages 2-10, before you begin to paint.

VEINED MARBLING FINISH

1. Basecoat the surface with Butter Cream; allow the paint to dry.
2. Mix Dark Foliage Green and glaze (1:1) on a foam plate. Dampen the surface with a light spritz of water. Pick up the mixture on a damp sea sponge, then begin stippling the surface. While the paint is still wet, spritz the stippled area with small amounts of water to blend the color outward (Fig. 13). Allow the paint to dry.

Instructions continued on page 28

FIG. 13

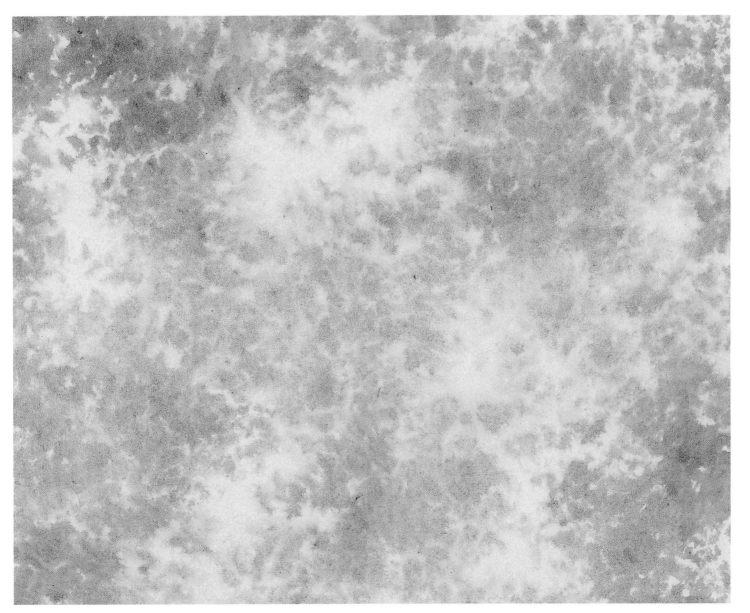

3. Spritz the surface with water again. Stipple the surface again with a heavier application of the green mixture from step 2. Mix Black and glaze (1:1) on a foam plate. Pick up the mixture on a damp sea sponge and, while the green areas are still wet, stipple small amounts of the black mixture over a few of the green areas to darken them (Fig. 14). Allow the paint to dry. This step will give your finish depth.

4. Roll on a layer of clear glaze and allow it to dry.
5. Mix Butter Cream and glaze (1:1) on a foam plate. Pick up a small amount of the mixture on a damp sea sponge. Dampen the surface with a spritz of water. Lightly stipple over some of the green areas with the cream mixture. Smudge the paint a little as you apply it (Fig. 15). Allow the paint to dry. Coat the surface with another layer of clear glaze and allow it to dry.

FIG. 14

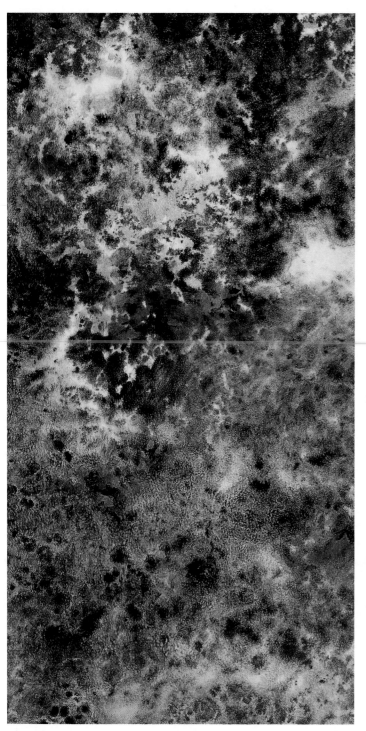

FIG. 15

6. Lightly dampen the surface with a spritz of water. Pick up water on a script brush and thin your black paint. Load the brush, then set the brush parallel to surface with the bristles touching the surface. Keeping in mind that veins normally move diagonally across marble, slowly begin to roll the brush between your index finger and thumb across the surface to create veining. Repeat to add Butter Cream veins (Fig. 16). Allow the paint to dry.

7. Dip a toothbrush in water and thin your black paint. Lightly speckle the surface. Repeat to speckle smaller areas of the surface with Butter Cream (Fig. 17, page 30). Allow the paint to dry.

8. Apply gloss varnish to your surface to produce a realistic, highly polished marble faux finish. Also, try creating this finish in shades of black, grey, and cream (Fig. 18, page 30).

FIG. 16

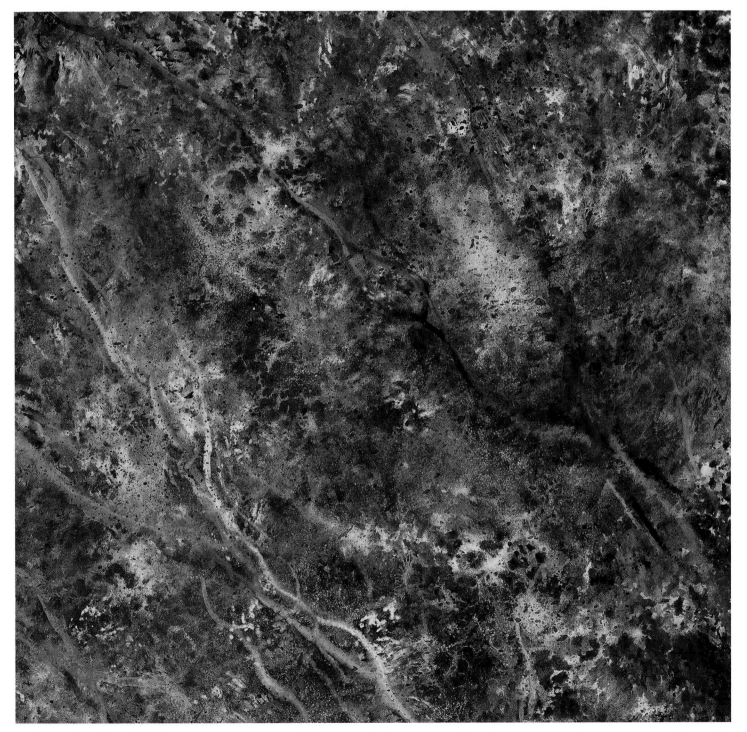

FIG. 17

FIG. 18

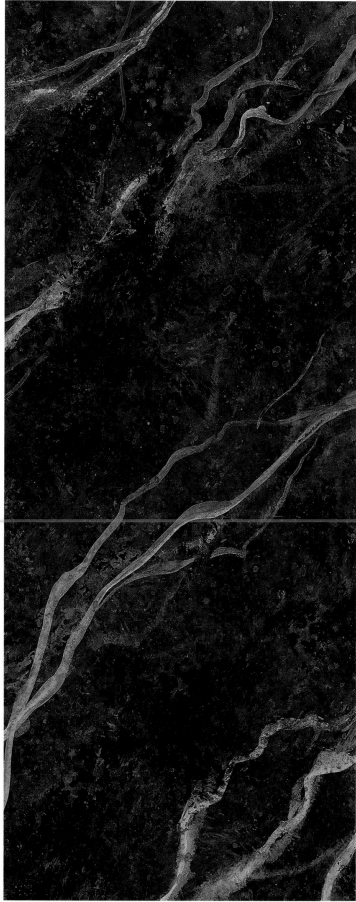

MOTTLED STONE

Two of the basic painting techniques are used to create the mottled stone finish. They are the paint removal technique using plastic wrap and stippling with a sponge.

PALETTE:

Delta Ceramcoat® Acrylics
Butter Cream
Candy Bar Brown
Pink Quartz
Raspberry

SUPPLIES:
Plastic wrap or plastic shopping bags

Read the General Painting Supplies and Basic Painting Techniques, pages 2-10, before you begin to paint.

MOTTLED STONE FINISH

1. Basecoat the surface with Candy Bar Brown; allow the paint to dry.
2. Mix Pink Quartz and glaze (1:1) on a foam plate. Brush a layer of the mixture onto the surface. Wrinkle up a piece of plastic. Open the plastic sheet and press it onto the surface, allowing wrinkles to form. Carefully remove plastic by lifting it straight up, then discard it. Repeat with clean pieces of plastic until the surface is covered with patterning (Fig. 1). Allow the paint to dry.

FIG. 1

Instructions continued on page 32

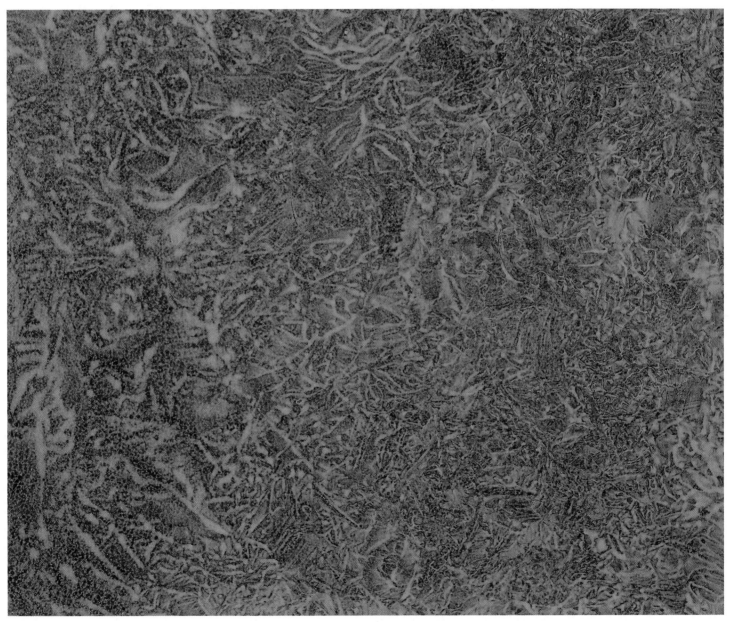

3. Mix Raspberry and glaze (1:1) on a foam plate. Use a chip brush to lightly apply the mixture to a damp kitchen sponge. Press sponge onto the surface in a few areas, then lift it straight up. Allowing the colors of the previously painted layers to show, repeat until the desired pattern is achieved (Fig. 2). This layer of your finish does not need to dry before you proceed to step 4.

4. You can now add additional layers of color to your finish. Begin by mixing Butter Cream and Pink Quartz (1:1) to create a lighter shade pink. Repeat step 3 with the light pink mixture (Fig. 3) and then with Butter Cream applied sparingly (Fig. 4). Remember – the desired effect is to see some color from every layer. Allow the paint to dry.

5. Try this technique with another color combination such as Autumn Brown with Palomino Tan, Brown Iron Oxide, and Chamomile (Fig. 5, page 34).

FIG. 2

FIG. 3

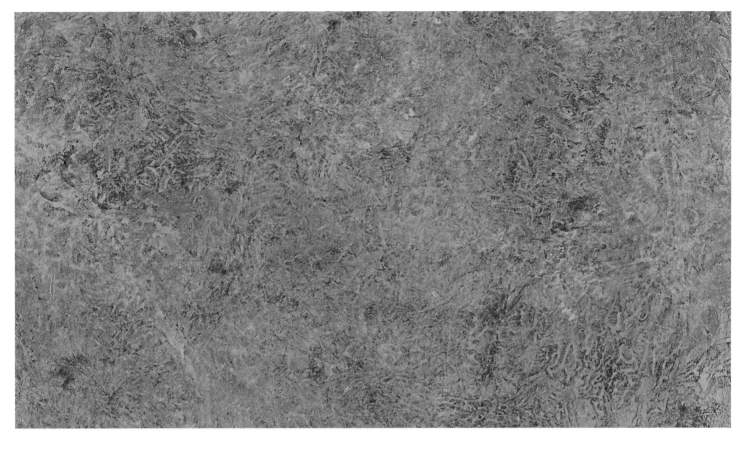

FIG. 4

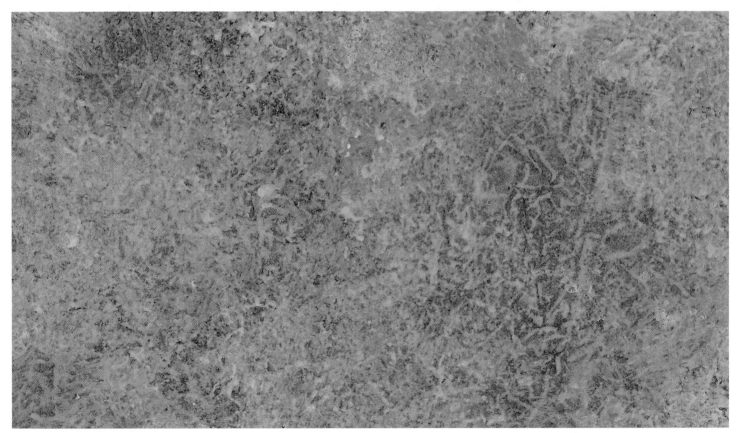

FIG. 5

POLISHED STONE

Many stones are taken from nature and then sliced and highly polished. They are extremely smooth. You can achieve this finish using the paint removal and sponging techniques.

PALETTE:

Delta Ceramcoat® Acrylics
Autumn Brown
Black
Brown Iron Oxide
Chamomile
Dark Victorian Teal

SUPPLIES:

Newspaper
Water bottle
Hair dryer

Read the General Painting Supplies and Basic Painting Techniques, pages 2-10, before you begin to paint.

POLISHED STONE FINISH

1. Basecoat the surface with Chamomile; allow the paint to dry.
2. Mix Autumn Brown, glaze, and water (1:1:1) on a foam plate. (The paint mixture will be an inky consistency.) Brush a layer of the mixture onto the surface. Dampen a piece of newspaper with water. Lay the wet newspaper paper onto the wet surface. Apply light pressure, then carefully remove the newspaper and discard it. Repeat with clean pieces of newspaper until the surface is covered with patterning. Hold hair dryer over surface to manipulate the position of your color and begin the drying process (Fig 1). Allow the paint to dry.

Instructions continued on page 36

FIG. 1

3. Additional colors now can be added in same manner as step 2. Begin with a layer of Dark Victorian Teal (Fig. 2) followed by a layer of Brown Iron Oxide (Fig. 3). These layers of color need to be extremely light. Allow each color layer to dry.
4. Roll on layer of clear glaze and allow it to dry.
5. Mix Chamomile, glaze, and water (1:1:2) on a foam plate. Pick up the mixture on a really wet sea sponge and stipple the wet surface. Now stipple a few areas with just Chamomile and some areas with Chamomile with a tiny amount of Black added (Fig. 4). Allow the paint to dry.
6. Try this technique with other color combinations, such as green with orange (Fig. 5, page 38) or plum with gold (Fig. 6, page 38). You can also add metallic colors and alcohol drops to this finish to create another interesting layer (Fig. 7, page 39). Finally, try adding a gold glaze over your surface to complete your finish (Fig. 8, page 39).

FIG. 3

FIG. 2

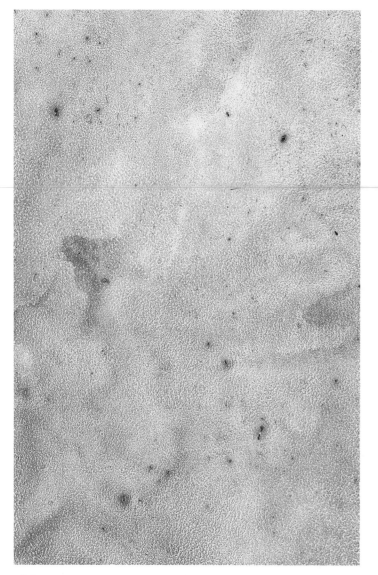

FIG. 4

FIG. 5

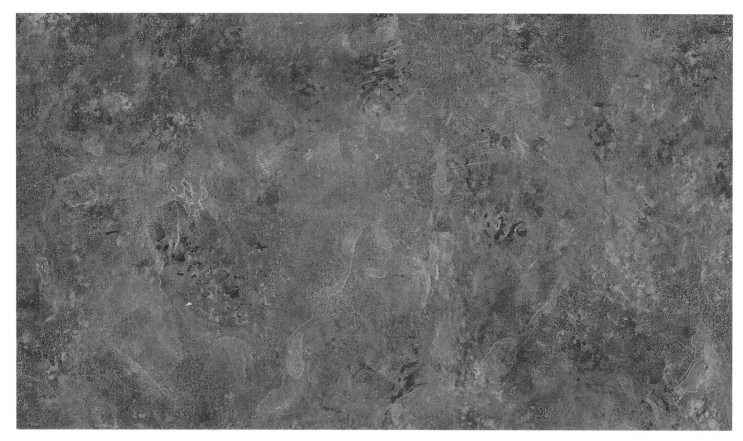

FIG. 6

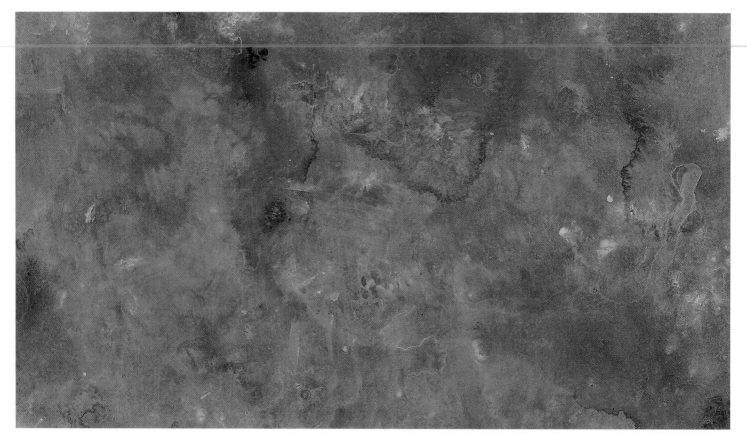

FIG. 7

FIG. 8

SMOOTH TEXTURE STONE

This finish is applied using several of the basic painting techniques including sponging, spritzing, and stippling.

PALETTE:
Delta Ceramcoat® Acrylics
Raw Sienna
Royal Plum
Spice Brown
Sweetheart Blush
Truly Teal

SUPPLIES:
Water bottle

Read the General Painting Supplies and Basic Painting Techniques, pages 2-10, before you begin to paint.

SMOOTH TEXTURE STONE FINISH

1. Basecoat the surface with Raw Sienna; allow the paint to dry.
2. Mix Spice Brown and glaze (2:1) on a foam plate. Pick up a small amount of the mixture on a damp sea sponge and stipple the surface randomly. Spritz the surface with water while the paint is still wet to soften the pattern. Note – the desired effect is blurry patterning. Allow the paint to dry.
3. Mix Royal Plum and glaze (2:1) on a foam plate. Pick up a small amount of the mixture on a damp sea sponge and lightly stipple the surface. Soften the color with a spritz of water (Fig. 1). Allow the paint to dry.
4. Roll on a layer of clear glaze and allow it to dry.
5. Add additional layers of color by repeating the stippling process using very small amounts of Sweetheart Blush, then Truly Teal (Fig. 2). If these colors become too heavy, let the surface dry, then stipple a little Spice Brown over the area and spritz with water to soften the colors (Fig. 3).

FIG. 1

FIG. 2

FIG. 3

OTHER *Finishes*

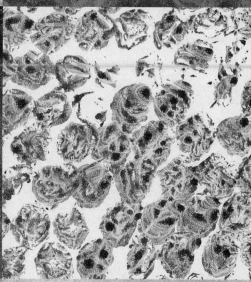

BUBBLE WRAP

Bubble wrap creates a busy, fun pattern. The size of the bubbles on the wrap will determine the texture pattern. I have used several of the basic painting techniques to complete the variations of this finish.

PALETTE:

Delta Ceramcoat® Acrylics
Butter Cream
Candy Bar Brown
Desert Sun Orange
Dunes Beige
Island Coral
Medium Victorian Teal

SUPPLIES:
Bubble wrap
Water bottle

Read the General Painting Supplies and Basic Painting Techniques, pages 2-10, before you begin to paint.

BUBBLE WRAP FINISH – DIRECT PAINT APPLICATION

1. Basecoat the surface with Butter Cream; allow the paint to dry.
2. Mix Candy Bar Brown and glaze (1:1) on a foam plate. Pick up the mixture on your paintbrush and lightly brush the mixture across the raised bubbles on a piece of bubble wrap. Place the bubble wrap, paint side down, on the surface. Gently press down on the bubble wrap, then remove the wrap; discard. If desired, lightly spritz the surface with water while the paint is still wet to soften the pattern (Fig. 1). Allow the paint to dry.

FIG. 1

Instructions continued on page 44

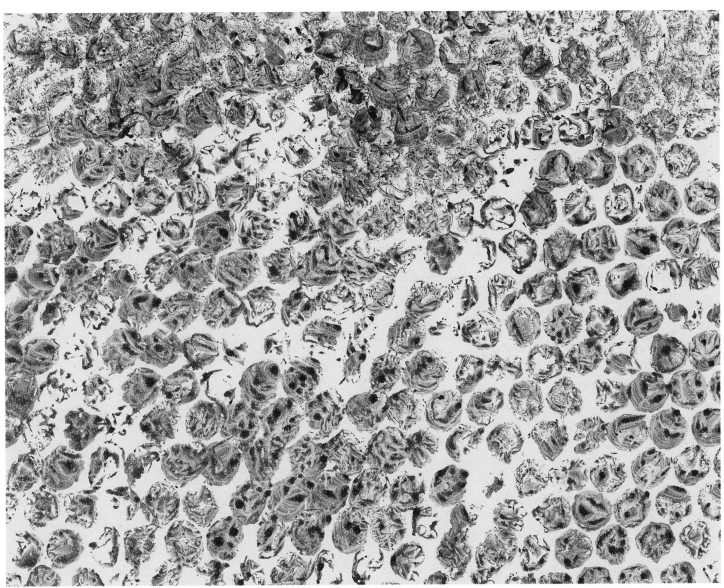

BUBBLE WRAP FINISH – PAINT REMOVAL

1. Basecoat the surface with Butter Cream; allow the paint to dry.
2. Mix Candy Bar Brown and glaze (1:1) on a foam plate. (Add a little water to the mixture if you would like a thinner, lighter color.) Pick up the mixture on your paintbrush and glaze over your surface. Take a piece of bubble wrap and press it into the wet glaze, then lift the wrap from the surface; discard. Allow the paint to dry.
3. Add an additional layer of color by mixing Dunes Beige and glaze (1:1) and repeating step 2 (Fig. 2). Allow the paint to dry.

FIG. 2

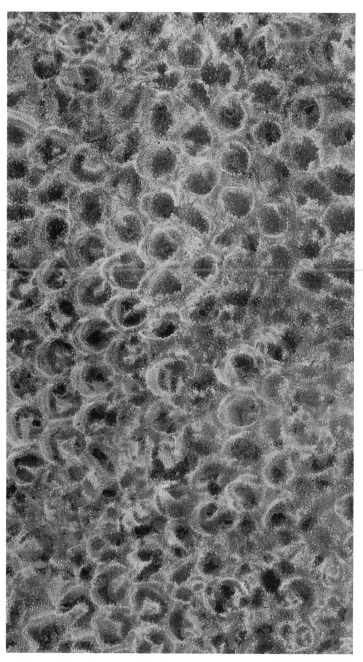

BUBBLE WRAP FINISH – MIXED

1. Basecoat the surface with Butter Cream; allow the paint to dry.
2. Mix Medium Victorian Teal and glaze (1:1) on a foam plate. Pick up the mixture on your paintbrush and lightly brush mixture across the raised bubbles on a piece of bubble wrap. Place the bubble wrap, paint side down, on the surface. Gently press down on the bubble wrap, then remove the wrap; discard. Allow the paint to dry.
3. Mix Island Coral and glaze (1:1) on a foam plate. Dampen a sea sponge. Pick up a small amount of mixture on the sponge and stipple the surface randomly. Lightly spritz the surface with water while the paint is still wet to soften the pattern. Allow the paint to dry.
4. Add an additional layer of color by mixing Desert Sun Orange and glaze (1:1) and repeating step 3 (Fig. 3). Allow the paint to dry.

FIG. 3

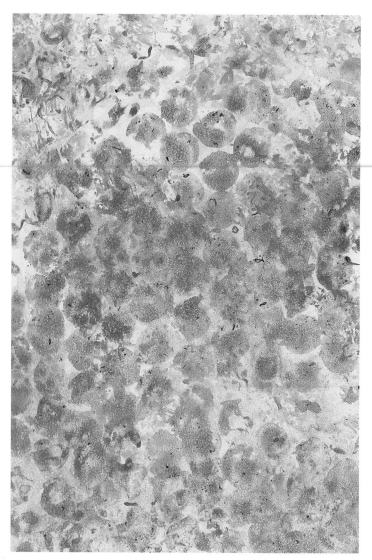

BURLED WOOD

Burled wood happens when buds on a tree mutate during early growth. They appear as bulges on the outside of a tree trunk and are usually not very large. When burled wood is used in furniture, it provides interesting accents with other wood grains. This finish appears very complicated but it's fun and easy to produce. The basic painting techniques used to complete this finish are sponging and spritzing. The other techniques used include manipulating some of the paint colors by adding glaze and water and adding brushed line work to the surface. This finish works best on small areas since you need to work fast and keep the surface wet while you are painting.

PALETTE:
Delta Ceramcoat® Acrylics
Antique Gold
Autumn Brown
Brown Iron Oxide
Dark Burnt Umber

SUPPLIES:
Newspaper
Water bottle

Read the General Painting Supplies and Basic Painting Techniques, pages 2-10, before you begin to paint.

FIG. 1

Instructions continued on page 46

BURLED WOOD FINISH

1. Basecoat the surface with Antique Gold; allow the paint to dry.
2. Lightly spritz the surface with water. Mix Autumn Brown, glaze, and water (1:1:1) on a foam plate. Pick up the mixture on a sea sponge. Stipple a few areas on the surface (Fig. 1, page 45). Spritz the wet paint with water. Mix Brown Iron Oxide, glaze, and water (1:1:2) on a foam plate. Pick up the mixture on a second sea sponge and stipple a few areas on the surface. Lightly spritz the surface with water again. Dampen some newspaper; press the damp newspaper on the wet paint. Carefully remove the newspaper and discard (Fig. 2). Be sure to keep the surface wet.

3. While the paint is still wet, scrunch some damp newspaper into a ball. Twist a few swirls into the wet paint on the surface (Fig. 3). Keep the surface damp, if possible.
4. While the paint is still wet, touch your index finger into thinned Dark Burnt Umber paint. Touch a little color in the center of a few of the swirled areas (Fig. 4). If the paint layers dry before you can get this done, spritz the dry surface with water, then apply the dark brown dots. Try to keep surface wet.

FIG. 3

FIG. 2

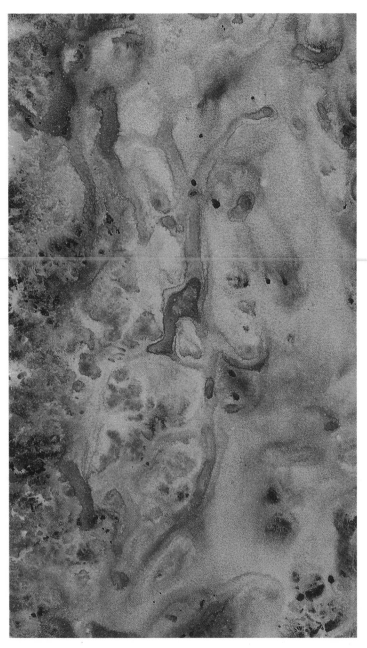

FIG. 4

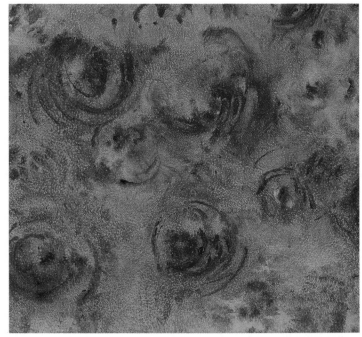

5. While the paint is still wet, thin Dark Burnt Umber with water. Use a script brush to create some curved lines around a few of the swirls (Fig. 5). Soften the lines with a clean, damp sea sponge, if needed. If the paint layers dry before you can get this done, spritz the dry surface with water, then apply the lines. Allow the paint to dry.

6. Sometimes a finish needs a warm tone glazed on top to complete the "look." Mix a sheer glaze with Antique Gold, glaze, and water (1:2:2). Apply the mixture evenly over the dry surface with a chip brush (Fig. 6, page 48). Allow the paint to dry.

FIG. 5

FIG. 6

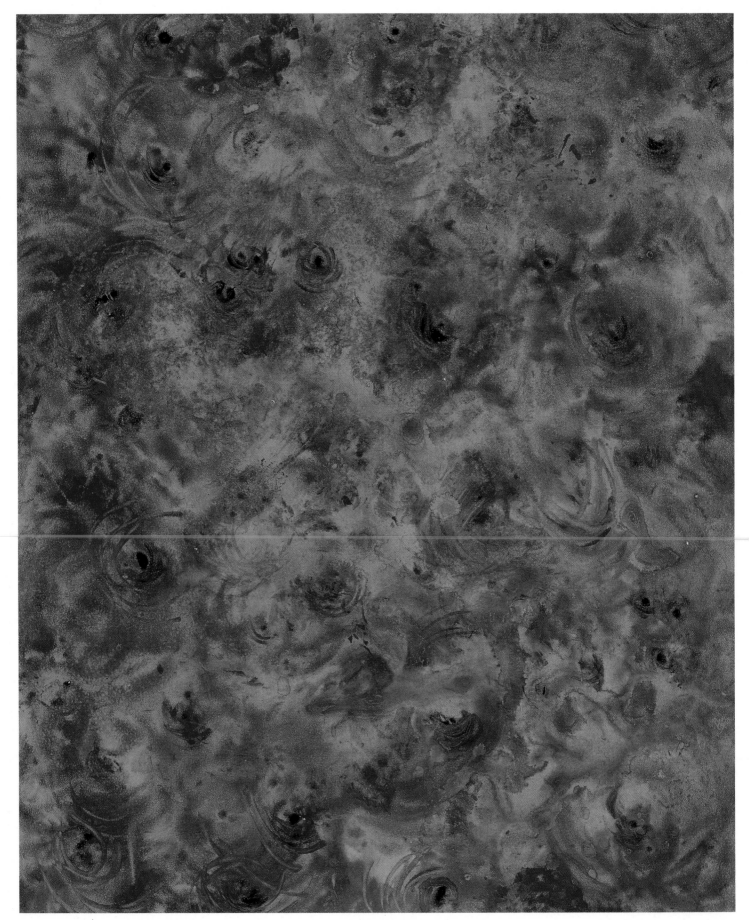

SMOOTH LEATHER

Leather may be duplicated using a variety of the basic painting techniques. I used the stippling technique in this book. I also manipulated some of the paint colors by adding glaze to them.

PALETTE:

Delta Ceramcoat® Acrylics
Autumn Brown
Chamomile
Medium Flesh

Read the General Painting Supplies and Basic Painting Techniques, pages 2-10, before you begin to paint.

SMOOTH LEATHER FINISH

1. Basecoat the surface by stippling it with Chamomile; allow the paint to dry.
2. Mix Autumn Brown and glaze (1:1) on a foam plate. (Add a little more glaze to the mixture if you would like a lighter, more transparent color.) Lightly dip the tip of a paintbrush into a small amount of the mixture and lightly stipple the surface. Be sure to leave areas of basecoat color visible. Use a clean brush dipped in a small amount of glaze to blend the edges of the patterns to soften (Fig. 1). Allow the paint to dry.
3. Repeat step 2 using Medium Flesh (Fig. 1). Be careful not to over blend your color layers. If this happens, allow the paint to dry and repeat steps 1-3 to repair areas and complete finish (Fig. 2, page 50).

FIG. 1

FIG. 2

TEXTURED *Finishes*

PAPER FINISHES

Papers are produced in many weights and textures. Papers may be mounted to surfaces as a texturing aid and may be applied over a white or a colored basecoat. Mounting paper to walls becomes a concern if removal is a future possibility. Use wallpaper paste instead of glaze to mount paper to walls. I use tissue and brown craft papers in this book.

TISSUE PAPER FINISHES

Some papers, such as tissue paper, are very thin and become fragile when wet. Be sure to handle tissue paper carefully.

PALETTE:

Delta Ceramcoat® Acrylics
Aquamarine
Autumn Brown
Chamomile
Dark Victorian Teal
Medium Flesh

SUPPLIES:

white tissue paper (or aqua tissue paper for the colored finish)

Read the General Painting Supplies and Basic Painting Techniques, pages 2-10, before you begin to paint.

MOUNTING TISSUE PAPER

1. Tear pieces of tissue paper into irregular shapes. Dampen the surface with glaze using a chip brush. Place the tissue paper pieces on the wet surface, overlapping the paper edges (Fig. 1). Now, brush another layer of glaze over the paper pieces, using light pressure on your brush to secure the bond. If the paper tears and a hole forms, cover the hole with more tissue paper. Allow the surface to dry.

WHITE TISSUE PAPER FINISH

1. Mount white tissue paper to surface. Mix glaze and Chamomile (1:1) on a foam plate. Stipple the mixture on the surface using a chip brush. Soften the pattern edges with a clean chip brush.
2. Repeat step 2 using Dark Victorian Teal (Fig. 2) and then using Autumn Brown (Fig. 3). Blend the color edges with a clean chip brush (Fig. 4). Allow the paint to dry.

Instructions continued on page 54

FIG. 1

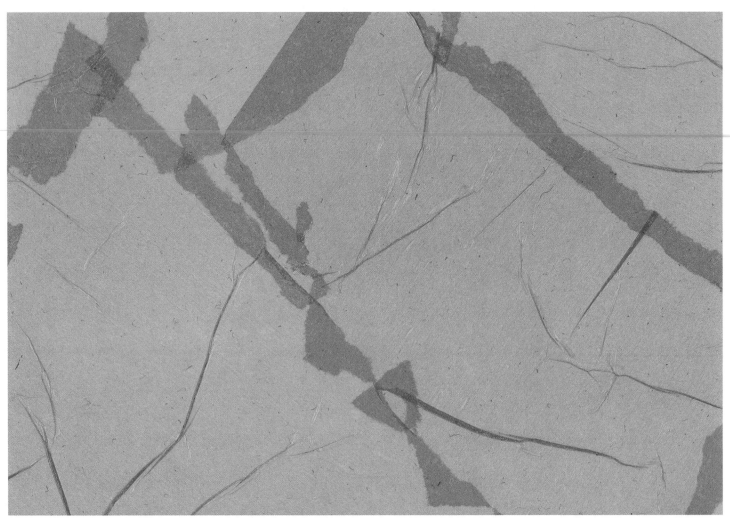

FIG. 2

FIG. 3

FIG. 4

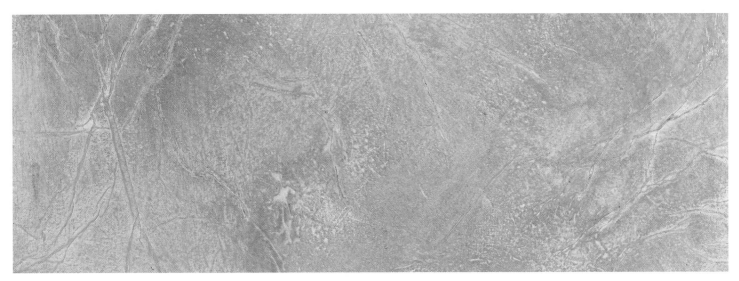

COLORED TISSUE PAPER FINISH

1. Mount aqua tissue paper to surface.
2. Follow step 2 of Tissue Paper Finish, page 52, to stipple surface with a glaze of Aquamarine, then with a glaze of Medium Flesh (Fig. 5). Blend the color edges with a clean chip brush and allow the paint to dry (Fig. 6).

FIG. 6

FIG. 5

WORN LEATHER PAPER FINISH

The worn leather finish can be produced by applying pieces of brown craft paper to your surface and dry brushing color over the surface.

PALETTE:

Delta Ceramcoat® Acrylics
Autumn Brown
Burnt Umber
Chamomile

SUPPLIES:

Brown craft paper

Read the General Painting Supplies and Basic Painting Techniques, pages 2-10, before you begin to paint.

WORN LEATHER PROCESS

1. Tear pieces of craft paper into irregular shapes. Mount the craft paper pieces to the surface using glaze or wallpaper paste, overlapping the paper edges to create more texture (Fig. 7). Seal the top of the surface with a layer of clear glaze and allow it to dry.
2. Mix Autumn Brown and glaze (1:1) on a foam plate. Also mix Burnt Umber and glaze (1:1) on a foam plate. Stipple some areas on the surface with Autumn Brown and some areas with Burnt Umber, leaving a lot of the paper unpainted. Blend the edges of the colors with a clean chip brush (Fig. 8).
3. Lightly dry brush over the surface with Chamomile (Fig. 9, page 56). Allow the paint to dry.

FIG. 7

FIG. 8

FIG. 9

RAISED TEXTURED FINISHES

Raised texture finishes are produced using a variety of tools and texturizing products. I use brush strokes, sponging, banded rolling, troweling, and paper application to achieve these finishes. You will also use dry brushing, paint removal, and direct application painting.

BRUSHSTROKE RAISED FINISH

This finish is formed by adding paint straight from the container with brushes or by brushing on a texture product. Allow 24 hours for the texture product to dry before completing finish.

PALETTE:

Delta Ceramcoat® Acrylics
Chamomile
Desert Sun Orange
Medium Victorian Teal

SUPPLIES:

Plastic scraper or trowel
All-purpose joint compound

FIG. 1

Read the General Painting Supplies and Basic Painting Techniques, pages 2-10, before you begin to paint.

BRUSHSTROKE RAISED FINISH – PAINT

1. Basecoat the surface with Desert Orange, applying pressure on the brush to form a texture on the surface with the bristles (Fig. 1). Allow the paint to dry.
2. Pick up a little Chamomile on the tip of the bristles of a dry chip brush and dry brush a layer of color on the surface until desired amount of texture is achieved (Fig. 2). Keep towels handy to wipe excess paint from the brush and remember that dry brushing is a layer building process. Allow the paint to dry.

Instructions continued on page 58

FIG. 2

BRUSHSTROKE RAISED FINISH – JOINT COMPOUND

1. Apply joint compound to the surface using a plastic scraper or trowel. Use a chip brush to spread the joint compound and form brush strokes. Allow the surface to dry.
2. Apply a layer of clear glaze to the surface and allow it to dry.

3. Mix Medium Victorian Teal, glaze, and water (1:2:1) on a foam plate. Pick up some of the mixture on a sea sponge. Lightly stipple over the surface (Fig. 3). Allow the paint to dry.
4. Repeat step 3 using Desert Sun Orange to add another layer of color to your finish (Fig. 4). Allow the paint to dry.

FIG. 3

FIG. 4

RAISED TEXTURE FINISH WITH SPECIAL EFFECTS

Use alcohol and salt to alter the painted surfaces and create exciting textures.

PALETTE:
Delta Ceramcoat® Acrylics
Aquamarine
Black Green
Butter Cream
Candy Bar Brown
Royal Plum

SUPPLIES:
Rubbing alcohol
All-purpose joint compound
Kosher salt

Read the General Painting Supplies and Basic Painting Techniques, pages 2-10, before you begin to paint.

Raised Texture Finish with Special Effects

1. Roll a layer of joint compound onto the surface and allow it to dry.
2. Now roll on a layer of clear glaze onto the surface and allow it to dry.
3. Basecoat the surface with Butter Cream; allow the paint to dry.
4. Mix Aquamarine, glaze, and water (1:2:1) on a foam plate. Pick up some of the mixture on a sea sponge. Lightly stipple over the surface. Allow the paint to dry.
5. Mix Candy Bar Brown and glaze (1:1) on a foam plate. Thin the mixture to an inky consistency with water. Brush the thinned mixture on the surface. Use a toothbrush to speckle the surface with alcohol (Fig. 5). Light speckling will create a fine texture, while larger drops of alcohol will create a more cratered appearance. Place a damp sponge on the surface if you would like to remove some of the color. Allow the paint to dry.
6. Mix Black Green and glaze (1:1) on a foam plate. Use a chip brush to apply the mixture to the surface. Use a toothbrush to speckle the surface with alcohol (Fig. 6).
7. Try using other techniques with this finish. Add another layer of thinned paint color and manipulate the color with a hair dryer. Use salt along with the alcohol to add even more interest (Fig. 7).

FIG. 5

FIG. 6

FIG. 7

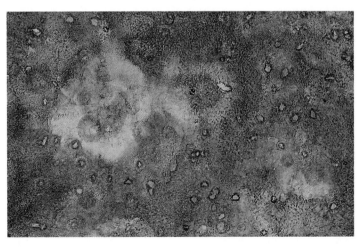

STUCCO FINISHES

Sponging or rolling texture products onto your surface will create a stucco finish. You will use stippling to complete these finishes.

SPONGING STUCCO FINISH
PALETTE:
Delta Ceramcoat® Acrylics
Autumn Brown
Chamomile
Medium Flesh

SUPPLIES:
All-purpose joint compound

Read the General Painting Supplies and Basic Painting Techniques, pages 2-10, before you begin to paint.

SPONGING STUCCO FINISH

1. Roll a layer of joint compound onto the surface, then stipple the surface with a damp sea sponge to create texture. Allow the surface to dry.
2. Now, roll a layer of clear glaze onto the surface and allow it to dry.
3. Basecoat the surface with Chamomile; allow the paint to dry.
4. Mix Medium Flesh and glaze (1:1) on a foam plate. Stipple the mixture on a few areas using a chip brush. Blend the paint edges with a clean chip brush loaded with a little clear glaze to aid in smoothing out the color (Fig. 1).
5. Repeat step 4 using Autumn Brown (Fig. 1). Allow the paint to dry to complete the finish (Fig. 2).

FIG. 1

FIG. 2

BANDED ROLLER STUCCO FINISH

A banded roller (see Banded Roller Marbling, page 19, for construction instructions) will produce a unique texture.

PALETTE:
Delta Ceramcoat® Acrylics
Candy Bar Brown
Chamomile

SUPPLIES:
All-purpose joint compound
Banded roller
Trowel or scraping tool

Read the General Painting Supplies and Basic Painting Techniques, pages 2-10, before you begin to paint.

BANDED ROLLER STUCCO FINISH

1. Roll a layer of joint compound onto the surface, then roll the banded roller across the surface to create texture. Allow the surface to dry.
2. Now, roll on a layer of clear glaze onto the surface and allow it to dry.
3. Mix Candy Bar Brown and glaze (1:1) on a foam plate. Brush the mix over the surface. While the paint is still wet, use a rag or paper towel to remove some areas of color (Fig. 3). Allow the paint to dry.
4. Repeat step 3 using Chamomile (Fig. 4). Allow the paint to dry.

FIG. 3

FIG. 4

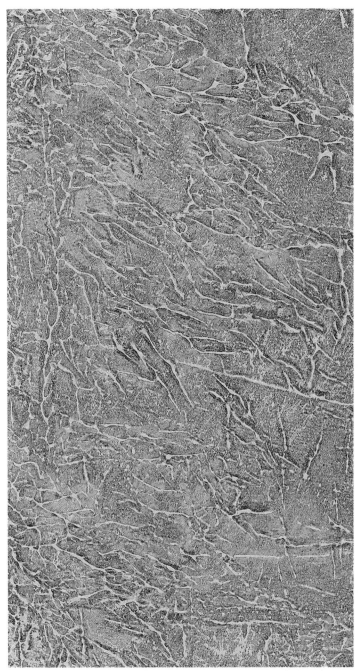

TROWELED FINISHES

Texture may be troweled onto a surface to create raised dimension. This finish is formed by adding paint straight from the container with brushes or by brushing on a texture product. The tools and products used will determine the texture. You can use old credit cards, scrapers, or trowels for your tools. Larger projects, such as walls, would benefit from using wall trowels.

PALETTE:

Delta Ceramcoat® Acrylics
Candy Bar Brown
Chamomile
Dark Victorian Teal

SUPPLIES:

Plastic scraper or trowel
All-purpose joint compound

FIG. 1

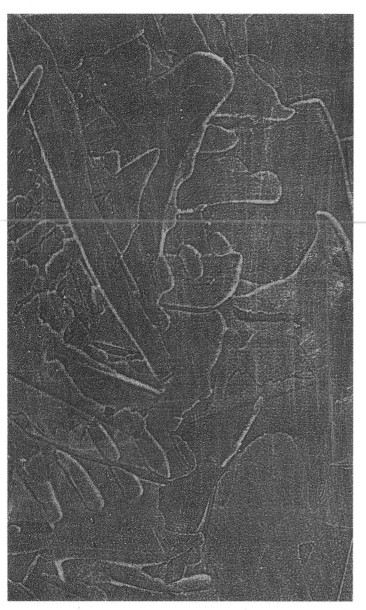

TROWELED FINISH – PAINT

1. Basecoat the surface with Chamomile. Use desired tool to spread a layer of Dark Victorian Teal across surface similar to frosting a cake, then skim across the wet paint to create a layer of texture (Fig. 1). Allow the paint to dry.
2. Add a second layer of color by dry brushing the surface with Chamomile (Fig. 2). Or, add an extra layer of color by applying a Chamomile glaze with a chip brush and then use a rag or paper towel to remove some of the color (Fig. 3).

FIG. 2

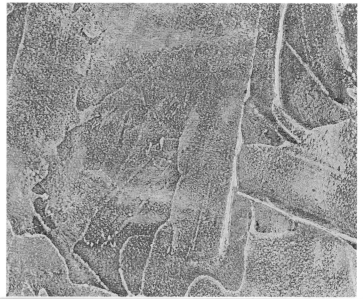

FIG. 3

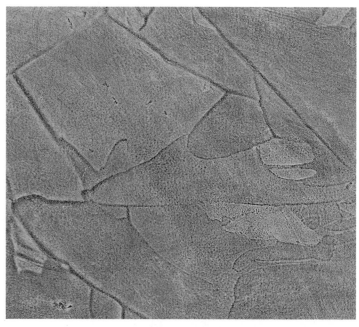

TROWELED FINISH – JOINT COMPOUND

1. Roll a layer of joint compound onto the surface, then trowel with the desired tool to create texture. Allow the surface to dry.
2. Now, roll a layer of clear glaze onto the surface and allow it to dry.
3. Basecoat the surface with Candy Bar Brown. Use a rag or paper towel to remove some of the color (Fig. 4).
4. Try this technique with other colors. You can achieve a nice brass finish by using a Black basecoat and then dry brushing the surface with metallic Bronze and metallic Gold (Fig. 5, page 64). A copper finish is done with a Dark Victorian Teal basecoat that is dry brushed with metallic Copper and metallic Bronze (Fig. 6, page 64).

FIG. 4

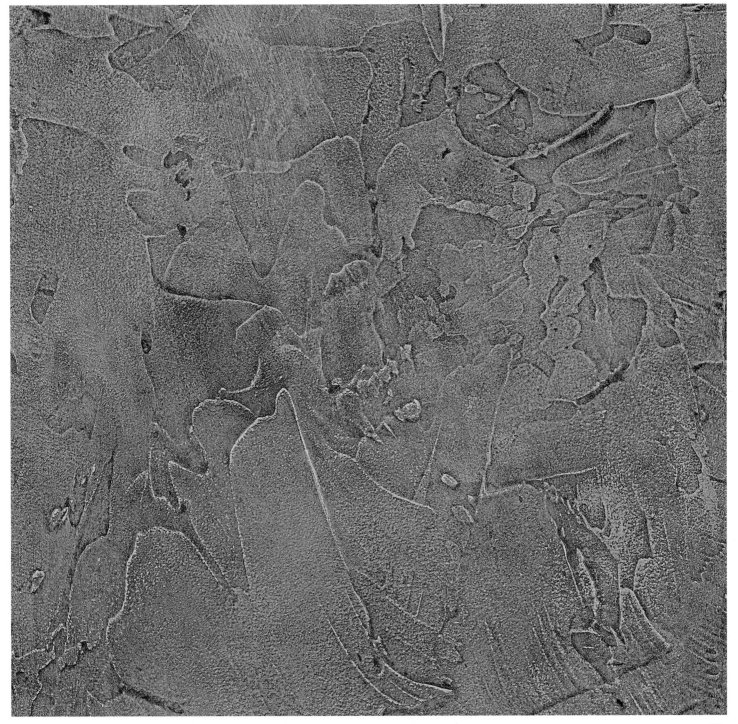

FIG. 5

FIG. 6